D1258398

ON
SPEAKING
OUT OF THE
SILENCE

*Vocal Ministry
in the
Unprogrammed
Meeting
for Worship*

by

DOUGLAS V. STEERE

PENDLE HILL PAMPHLET 182

About the Author / Douglas Steere joined the Religious Society of Friends by convincement in 1932. Coming to the Quakers after a period of religious quest, he has from the beginning been deeply appreciative of the mutation of the silent meeting for worship and its corporate waiting upon God. His little pamphlet, *A Quaker Meeting for Worship,* has gone through many editions and been widely used, enabling others to share in his experience of what takes place in worship of this type.

Having worshipped with Friends in nearly every part of the world, he has had occasion to be ministered to by many sorts of messages. He has served as Clerk of Ministry and Worship of Philadelphia Yearly Meeting from 1944-1947, and has taken an active share in the life and worship and ministry of Radnor Meeting at Ithan, Pennsylvania.

The present pamphlet has grown out of a paper given at the request of Radnor Meeting. This meeting makes a practice of using several forum sessions each year to reinterpret, for both members and attenders, the nature and functioning of the Friends' way of worship. This is done in order to increase the sense of expectancy, and to give a frame of interpretation to what is being done in the meeting for worship, in the meeting for business, in the vocal ministry, and in the personal preparation for these religious exercises. In revised and expanded form, this paper served as the opening address at an autumn meeting of the Meeting Workers Institute at Pendle Hill.

Requests for permission to quote or to translate should be addressed to Pendle Hill Publications, Wallingford, Pennsylvania 19086.

Copyright © March 1972 by Pendle Hill
Library of Congress catalog card number 72-182983

Printed in the United States of America by
Sowers Printing Company, Lebanon, Pennsylvania

1st printing March 1973 : 6,000
2nd printing July 1975 : 1,500

W E live in a time when we are especially conscious of the fact that there are many ministries and that the vocal ministry is only one of them. There are those who lean toward ministries of works, of involvement in the social and institutional problems of our time. There are those gifted in the ministry of writing, and others in the ministry of counselling. There is in fact no legitimate occupation that cannot in a certain sense be turned into a ministry. But I want here to explore afresh the very unusual way that the vocal ministry springs up in an unprogrammed Quaker meeting which settles itself in silent expectant waiting, and to look into ways that it can be sustained in a condition of health in such a meeting. While this exploration is directed very especially to the Quaker family who worship in this type of meeting, I believe there is a wider constituency who are deeply interested in the three centuries of corporate experience of this type of worship, and in the way in which a lay group is enabled to provide a prophetic ministry that may emerge from its silent worship of God.

I spent two months in the spring of 1969 at the Earlham School of Religion in Richmond, Indiana, and there I saw the effort that they were making to improve the quality of the vocal ministry in the pastoral meetings for which they feel a very special responsibility. Many Friends and others do not realize that well over two-thirds of the membership of the Society of Friends in the world today belong to meetings that are within the pastoral system, and that its vocal ministry is largely carried by trained pastors who are paid for their service or, as in the case of the meetings in East Africa where there is not enough money at hand to pay for many pastors, the vocal ministry comes largely from prearranged or programmed messages which men and women elders or others are asked in advance to give in meetings for worship.

I am not going to deal with these pastoral meetings here; they have another set of problems. But I am going to focus entirely upon the texture of the vocal ministry which comes up out of the silent, waiting, unprogrammed meeting that is grounded on the promise in the New Testament that "where two or three are gathered together in my name", the Emmaus experience will be reenacted.

There is a story of a Quaker who chided his Protestant minister friend about preparing his sermons in his study, urging him instead to trust the Holy Spirit and to go into his pulpit and have faith that what he was to say would be given to him there. The Protestant clergyman replied, "You old Quaker, don't you think that the Holy Spirit can inspire me at my desk in my study just as readily as it can reach you when you stand up on your hind legs in a silent Quaker meeting?" The Quaker replied, "Of course it can, but have you ever thought what the Devil has a chance to do with your sermons between the time you prepare them and when you deliver them? Now when a Quaker gets up to speak in meeting, the Devil himself doesn't know what he is going to say!" I am not going to emphasize the cunning concealment of our message from the Devil which this ancient Friend in his extremity drew from his quiver for defense against his clerical adversary, but the story does bring into focus what I think we who owe so much to the nurture of the unprogrammed meeting are prepared to trust and to explore. I believe that it is the faith that there is something going on in our silent waiting, something beyond our surface minds' capacity to grasp; that

4

there is a yearning communication that is continually operative; and that an unprogrammed silent meeting for worship is a wonderful climate for communication to break through; and that when vocal ministry comes out of this ground of communication and articulates it for the needs of those gathered together, conditions for inward transformation and strengthening are optimum indeed.

What is this yearning communication that was promised us and that we have from time to time experienced in our meetings? What is the Holy Spirit and how dare Quakers speak of a person of the Trinity when their theological training is so frail and their trust in theology almost non-existent?

Perhaps a non-professional theologian, Dorothy Sayers, a gifted English woman writer of the last generation, may help us here. She finds in the process of literary creation a metaphor for the action of the Trinity. Out of the mysterious and unplumbed and unplumbable depth of her imagination she draws a theme; she articulates it; and she is able to reach through to the mysterious depths of her readers. She believes that this act can shed more light than a whole shelf of SUMMAS on what is actually taking place in the Universe through the operations of what theologians call the "Trinity." From this root-metaphor of her experience of literary creation, she suggests that what the "persons" of the Trinity are trying to express is that the creative unplumbable abyss of the Godhead yearns itself forth as creator, that is, as God the Father; as the articulated message of redeeming love in the Son; and in the continuous communication within the unfathomable depths in men (and perhaps in every cell of creation as well) in the Holy Spirit.

Every page that she writes reenacts for her this metaphor and helps her to realize that at the ground of things there is a great sweep of communication that is going on now. Creation did not take place and stop. The appearance of a man who was a matchless window to this caring love did not enter history at a given point and then become simply a memory. The Holy Spirit

5

was not a dated possession of the Apostolic period. All three of these movements of the unfathomable Godhead are in continuous communication now. If we should apply this moving insight to the occasions when we are rightly gathered in the silence, then vocal ministry, frail as it may be, is one of the expressions of the operativeness here and now of this yearning, redemptive, transforming process.

Why then do we come here to sit together for our period of waiting expectant worship? We come because we, too, sense that something is going on all the time, something that we have only partially grasped the meaning of, and we long to be brought more deeply into touch with it. We come because in our kaleidoscopic lives with so many priorities all simultaneously demanding the first place in us, we dimly sense that there is, communicating with us in broken ways throughout the week, something, Someone, that could make us one again. The *Imitation of Christ* witnesses to what we long for when it says that "He in whom the Eternal Word speaks, is delivered from many opinions." And Augustine in his *Confessions,* reporting to us on his own experience, says, "I was collected from the dispersion in which I turned from Thee, the One, and was vainly divided."

We come to our meetings for worship because we suspect that this communication may help us to discern what is being asked of us in the way of suitable action in the situation in which we stand and because we need strengthening in the power to carry this out. "Did thee yield? Was thee faithful?" were two central personal Quaker queries that mirror this human need that draws us. Again out of his deeply tested experience, Isaac Penington witnesses to his own assurance that "There is that near you which will guide you; O wait for it and be sure ye keep to it." The demand for attention and for obedience which Thomas Mann says exhausts the heart of the highest religious quest are both there in this pull that brings us to the waiting meeting.

We come, too, for healing and forgiveness and renewal. And perhaps, back of it all, there is a craving to express our thanks for the very existence of this possibility, the very thrust of this communication from One who is forever caring and One who will not let us go.

We do not, however, come alone to the meeting. For the needs of those within and without the meeting sit down with us. They sit down with us in the person of our bodies which connect us with the whole of the natural creation and every exchange of breath reveals our profound dependence on the rest of nature and discloses to us our responsibility for it. They sit down with us in the persons of those who actually sit on the benches with us, each of whom is the center of a world of his own and who yearns as I do for the great tendering, the new angle of vision, the regrouping within, that would respond to the deepest thing that we know. They sit down with us, the wretched and the poor of the earth, both in spirit and in body, and a new feeling sense of our unity with them may be opened in that sitting.

It is in this climate that we enter the unprogrammed meeting for worship. And with few further references to this climate of receptivity, I will turn to the sharing of what is discovered in such a meeting as it reveals itself in its vocal ministry. I will try to be as blunt and as personal and practical as I can.

I might begin by confessing that there are some persons who attend a Friends' meeting for worship with the hope that there will be no vocal ministry at all. They prefer the silence, and resent messages of vocal ministry as intrusions. I suppose that in a certain sense all of us have these moments when we would rather not be disturbed. But the actual truth of the matter is that meetings that have turned completely silent almost inevitably wither away. Something is missing in the corporate relationship. The same thing is true even in a retreat that is conducted with the retreatants keeping complete silence. Most persons desperately want a session at the close of the retreat where some report can be made right round the board on what has been taking place and what has been breaking through in the lives of the others, and it is a sound instinct. This does not mean that an occasional completely silent meeting may not be one in which great things have happened within the hearts of those who attended. But the practical experience of the Society of Friends, historically, knows the fate of a meeting that is habitually mute.

Friends have from the outset taken seriously the New Testament injunction that all believers are priests. That is, they are to be vehicles of communication to each other in a redemptive community in which we have, in fact, abolished the laity and are all ministers. If this is true then no one should come to meeting quite certain that he will not speak. "Let none of us assume that vocal ministry is never to be our part" is what the Advices say. It is our feeling that it is equally unfortunate if someone comes in advance quite certain that he or she *will* minister. Rather we are meant to come to meeting in openness.

There is a classic passage in John William Graham's *The Faith of a Quaker* that is to be found in a chapter with the suggestive subtitle, "The Workshop of the Ministry." Here is what he says about the way a message comes to him in a meeting for worship: "It comes in waiting. When I sit down in meeting I recall whatever may have struck me freshly during the past week . . . so thoughts suggest themselves—a text that has smitten one during the week (it is interesting to note that he has been reading his Bible during the week)—new light on a phrase, a verse of poetry—some incident, private or public. These pass before the door whence shines the heavenly light. Are they transfigured? Sometimes, yes: sometimes, no. If nothing flames, silence is my portion. I turn from ideas of ministry to my private needs. From these, sometimes the live coal from off the altar is brought, suddenly and unexpectedly, and speech follows. Sometimes it does not. Again there are times when the initial thought strikes in of itself from the Inner Man beyond the will. These are times to be thankful for. Often two or three of the thoughts that have struck home during the week are woven together and in unexpected ways. When the fire is kindled, the blaze is not long. In five minutes from its inception, the sermon is there, the heart beats strongly and up the man must get. How trying is any outward interruption during these rapt and fruitful minutes when the whole scheme is unfolding itself, and flashing itself upon the brain. There are the five or six points, the leading sequences of thought are there, the expository teaching, the generalization, the illustrations, the final lesson and appeal, then fall into place. The sermon is made, but I the slow compiler did not make it." (pp. 245-6)

In this finely-drawn account of John William Graham's experience, there is strangely missing either any reference to his felfow worshippers that refers to their needs, or to the ministry of the fellow-worshippers that may well have preceded his own. Both of these considerations would seem to me to be of first importance in the very inner workshop of ministry itself, for ministry that is lastingly helpful is always deeply aware of the people who are gathered together for the meeting for worship. It is, of course, true that if I minister to my own deep need and share something that has spoken to my own condition, it is likely to meet the needs of many others in the room, for our conditions are not so different as many of us tend to think they are. Again and again when I have shared some ministry that spoke to my own need and struggle, someone has come up to me after the meeting and said, "You must have known that you were speaking directly to me." Yet after this has been said, ministry is often much strengthened if the one ministering knows something of the problems and the heartaches and the brave living that is going on in the room. This cannot be easily known except as the one ministering knows the people personally and has some real touch with them outside of the meeting.

I was asked recently to give the homily or sermon at the Roman Catholic Mass in a Benedictine House just outside of Madison, Wisconsin. I had been leading an ecumenical retreat there during the week-end and the retreatants, together with the Benedictine sisters and the other guests, were all present at the Mass. The night before, a Roman Catholic woman retreatant who was in her thirties had come to see me and told me that she was in the last stages of cancer and had only a few months to live. She had been battling it for two years now, had had cobalt, and was under heavy medication. She had a husband and five little boys, the oldest of whom was eight, and leaving them was not easy. She told me, however, that she had come through, and that prayer in her weakness was what she had lived from. She had rested her weight on it and it had held her up. When I found on coming back to my room that night that the set passage of the Gospels for the Mass the next morning that I was to speak on was the raising of Lazarus from the dead, I was searched to the core, knowing the situation of this woman, knowing that I was in physical strength and that she was ever so close to that Lazarus scene. As I spoke the next morning I was searched every moment and in every word that I said both by the need and by the magnificent witness of this woman. In a meeting for worship in a redemptive community which the Society of Friends is meant to be, the human situation of the community is a real factor in the communication.

I mentioned also that there was no reference in this fine passage from Graham to the ministry that had gone before, although at other places in the book this is not wholly neglected. The assumption in this passage, however, is that the message seems to have been formed and given without any connection to the other ministry that may already have come in the meeting. For one who speaks early in the meeting or who is the first to break the silence, this description might well fit, but most ministry is given in some connection with the ministry of others.

I have never felt easy about the description of William Penn coming into a meeting and beginning to speak before he had barely taken his seat. Most seasoned ministry comes out of a gathered meeting and a meeting may take some little time to be gathered. My own personal experience is that our swift three-quarters of an hour meeting is all too brief for effective ministry, for I must confess that I tend to speak late in the meeting and that it takes me some time to be settled, to feel into the inward exercise of the meeting, and to face what is being said in and through us. This does not mean that I have not, like John William Graham, often come with some special concerns or experiences or perhaps the seed of something that I might share if way opened for it in meeting. But these are more often than not laid aside or incorporated in the new situation that the previous ministry has both created and reflected, so that something quite new and different is formulated in my mind.

I think that learning to move in the exercise of the meeting so that one is a part of it, yet taken beyond it and brought to see some new light as a result of it, is most important in creative ministry. The cluster of messages, with a fair interval of silence between each of them to let its insight sink in; the cluster that goes on down, with each message deepening and intensifying and helping to light up a further facet of the communication, can be most effective. But for this to happen, those sharing in it cannot be in a discussional frame of mind, or in a debating stance, or yield to the ruthlessly critical mind, or all is lost and the meeting is pulled into a forum. It can only be done if there is a willingness to be led by each of the ones ministering into a deeper level of what they were not only saying but what they were meaning to say, and perhaps even beyond into what something beneath us all was meaning to have said through what we were saying and were meaning to say. When a cluster ministry moves in this way, we all know that we are moving in the life, that we are breaking the cerebral barrier and being released, that our greatest need is being met and we rejoice or we are convicted or we are ourselves ignited into flame by what is taking place.

If there is One who gathers the meeting inwardly and who is communicating and drawing at our lives unceasingly, and if vocal ministry in such a meeting is focused and irradiated from a level below the surface mind, it should not surprise us if several persons in the meeting were at the same time moved to minister on, roughly, the same theme. I have, on too many occasions to make it seem merely a coincidence, felt drawn to share a message and been startled to find another rising and ministering on almost the same theme, using of course other words and other illustrations than I would have used, but saying essentially the same thing and relieving me of the responsibility to minister. I have also been approached many times after meeting by two or three persons and told that if I had not risen first to minister, as I had done, they would have felt they must do it, for they had felt the exercise of the meeting draw their minds to almost the identical accent and they often thanked me for relieving them of this duty. The workshop of the vocal ministry in an unprogrammed meeting when we are brought into its inner chamber is alert with power and wonders. Yet with deeper faith such miracles should be expected.

One or two other small comments occur to me in connection with the passage which was quoted from John William Graham. It is clear that he is used to speaking in meeting and that he has none of the hesitations about breaking into speech that may be hindering many in the meeting from speaking, even when they are inwardly bidden to do so. When he says, "The heart beats strongly and up the man must get," it all sounds so simple. John Fothergill, although he wrote the following words in 1697, speaks for many today: "When the time came indeed that I was to open my mouth in a few words for the Lord among his people it was so indisputably clear, that I had no scruple about its being certainly the holy requiring: and yet in fear I reasoned it away . . ." When he finally did give in to it, he speaks of leaving the meeting with "a holy peace of mind." Some resist week after week until they finally, in defeat, resolve that they will never speak in meeting and delegate the matter to others.

It is next to impossible to touch on the personal hesitations before the call to minister without noting that the great freedom of the unprogrammed Quaker meeting may tempt some persons to minister too frequently, or be used for self expression by some distraught persons, or by some who have attended the meeting very seldom but who take this as an invitation to press some personal cause. It is amazing how much of this kind of speaking a strong meeting can absorb and can take down into the silence. Often this silence and its subsequent ministry can transform it into something unbelievably helpful. The confrontations that some meetings have had from black groups that have intruded what they had to say into the meeting itself, have, after the first startled condition of shock, often resulted in amazing revelations of insight for the scarification and deepening of the meeting.

This is not the place to discuss the whole matter of eldering that needs rethinking in the permissive mood that exists in most of our meetings at this time. But there are still times when in order to save a meeting from persistent disruption or distress, some quiet and loving conferring with those whose ministry is unhelpful must be undertaken.

Equally important is the raising of the question at least, of whether ministry in our time has not tended to neglect the great human existential questions: "From where did I come? Why am I here? Whence am I bound?" The nature of Friends' ministry is such that speaking to these great issues must come from the depths of the meeting's inward exercise and be experientially grounded. But when in the life, Friends have spoken to man's deepest needs and have never been content to confine ministry to moral preachments.

When John William Graham speaks of his "five or six main points," he also gives away the fact that he is used to a very considerable confidence in his being able either to discover or to remember that many! For the one often torn by inward struggles who has been drawn to speak, there may be nothing but a broken burst, or a prayer or a snatch of a question which he or she may get out in early attempts to minister. This can be of immeasurable benefit to a meeting. William Dewsbury wrote to encourage the simple ministry in his words from prison in York Tower in 1660: "And thou, faithful babe, though thou stutter forth a few words in the dread of the Lord, they are accepted." A 1949 Advice coming from London Yearly Meeting puts the matter admirably: "If the call comes, there should be no quenching of the spirit; the sense of unworthiness must not exempt us from the service, nor the fear of being unable to find the right words. . . . Broken and imperfect words springing from the deep place in the heart may wonderfully draw those present into communion with God and with one another."

My own experience would also confirm a remark of Graham's, which I mean to quote later on, where he describes the need for pruning one's messages. For me, the dropping away of surplus illustrations or peripheral considerations frequently takes place, sometimes willingly and sometimes with pain. When one is in the life, brevity is often given to the message. Chesterton's word about the blessedness of the power of the veto is a good thing to keep freshly in the mind. William Bacon Evans once sat through a half hour message from one Friend in a Yearly Meeting session on Temperance. When the Friend finally sat down, Bacon rose and said, "If some Friends would use temperance in their speaking, others would not have to practice total abstinence!" John William Graham reports the same reflections in his additional word, "Do I then always say what I intend and no more? Generally, a good deal less. Constantly the restraining influence of the Guide stops my saying all that I meant, or half meant to say, and rarely have I regretted the omissions. . . . Again does one never expand when one is speaking? Yea, verily. But mind your Guide here. This practice needs particular caution. Do not limit the spirit to its working before you rise (he knows how the Divine Listener often queries what is being said even while it is being uttered); but limit your own faculties of utterance, particularly if you have been in the habit of speaking for many years." (*The Faith of a Quaker* p. 247) I would add that it may

14

well be that we cannot finish, but we can always stop!

There is, in fact, such a thing as ministry that can be so finished and rounded off that members may hesitate to attach other messages to it. A young college teacher told me about a teacher whom we both knew and said that when he had finished taking one of this man's courses, he decided then and there that he could never be a teacher in that field because this teacher had done everything there was to do and all he could do would be to repeat him! Perhaps if not "five or six" but even one or two main points can be touched upon—and the ministering Friend sit down, the very openness or the one-sidedness or the angularity of what was said may be the very thing that will draw out others to complete it in a way that the speaker could never himself have done.

Should controversial social or economic or contemporary situations be brought into the ministry of the meeting, or do these belong in the forum or in some especially appointed meeting to deal with them? I think that Howard Brinton has given a wise if difficult-to-follow-out counsel on this issue. "An academic discussion of economic problems would interfere with the spirit of worship, but a solemn reverent appeal for greater sensitivity of conscience in economic matters might deepen the meeting" *(Guide to Quaker Practice,* pp. 18-19).

Berdyaev once said that "bread for myself is an economic problem" but that "bread for my brother is a spiritual problem," and meetings for worship would be poor indeed if they excluded such prophetic insights. It is possible, however, for Friends to outrun their Guide, and to be misled into identifying their own current resolution of social issues with Divine truth, and to evidence a condemnatory edge for all who do not share their views. Ministry of this vein is seldom helpful in a meeting for worship.

In ministry, to lay an issue before the deepest insight of the meeting, to take it to God and have it held there, to wait for the

Guide and to be content to have the melting-down process that can take place in a gathered meeting do its work: this kind of exercise, far from intruding on worship, can only strengthen it. But meeting for worship is not a forum for pressing fixed opinions.

What happens when something that has been shaped up in your mind in meeting does not seem to you right to be shared at this time? This often takes place. The Quaker journals have confirmed for me my own experience on two other matters: the first is that some things are given me for myself and not for sharing in the meeting: things that *I* am to follow out, things that *I* am to try to put right, things that *I* must test out in my own attempt to fulfill them before I am at liberty, if I ever am, to share them with others. The second matter the journals confirm is that to receive a message itself in meeting is not the same as to receive the call to give it, and that these are separate and distinguishable stages. When Phillip Neri says, "O Lord, keep a firm hand on Phillip today," the word might well be spoken by one who often ministers in meeting.

A further question may arise as to what happens to a message that has come but that one has not been at liberty to share. My own experience has been that nothing is ever lost. It may not have been matured, not shaken down as yet. It may first have to be tested by my own conduct to see if I mean it. It may have been given me for some other occasion. If the firm hand on me has not given it release, that does not mean that the disclosure is either meaningless or that it will not in some as yet undisclosed way be put to use.

There are instances in Quaker history of the reverse of this where a visiting ministering Friend has returned to a meeting for three weeks in a row and not feeling released from his obligation has repeated the identical message. I know some who would have referred the matter to the Committee for the Care of Confused Friends, but in this particular instance it is authentically reported that at the third meeting a person was present for whom this message was the occasion for the changing of his life.

The climate of a meeting does much to condition the freedom of the communication in ministry. The critical, frosty, overly-sensitive or divided meeting has a way of inhibiting ministry. The old habit of Protestant church attenders serving well-roasted and carved-up sermons with the Sunday dinner is not entirely unknown to Friends and does not improve the climate of receptivity. A great deal of charity is needed about messages that come in the meeting. No message is likely to be meant for every one of the worshippers. What may not affect me, may open out life for another, and this consciousness must always be there. Unamuno's sharp word about Goethe's alleged dying words may be well known to you where he said, "What we need is not 'Light, light, more Light' but warmth, warmth, more warmth, for we die not of the darkness but of the frost." Tender plants are easily wilted by the frost. We do indeed need warmth and a deep climate of acceptance of each other.

The matter of encouraging those who have ministered helpfully and acceptably is a delicate affair among Friends. The word that the message was especially helpful need not draw from most persons what it once did from a testy Friend whose reply to such a compliment was only, "That is exactly what the Devil said to me as I sat down after ministering." The most enduring encouragement comes from within, but a gentle pat on the arm by someone who has felt the flow of the spirit in the message has not been found to corrupt most Friends and in more than one instance has drawn them to be more open for future service in the vocal ministry of the meeting.

On the whole matter of preparation for meeting ministry, the word of an old veteran is revealing who, when asked how long it took him to prepare that message, replied that it had taken about sixty-five years of living. There is no standard preparation, no standard age, no standard sex. The early Friends were critical of the clergy who had been prepared at Oxford and Cambridge, but their protest was not levelled so much at the universities as at these clerics' habit of preaching less from their *own* experience of the power of the Holy Spirit in the life of their time than from the written accounts of the experiences of others.

In the most effective preparation for vocal ministry, the Bible is a powerful help. I like the African Christian's confession to his pastor that "It is not I that am reading the Bible, but it is the Bible that is reading me." *To be read by the Bible* as one confronts it day by day is to be made more open for a ministry of power. For if the Bible is not a record of universal human experience and of that experience being lifted onto another level —then it is not what we have believed it to be. Quakers have never made the Bible their only authority, but have always insisted that it is only as we are brought into the same spirit that gave forth the Bible that we can begin to understand it.

How should one prepare his mind and spirit for ministry? There have been places and times when Quakers have been sceptical about higher education as a preparation for ministry. Told that God had no use for his learning, a widely-read Friend inquired quietly if he had any greater use for his admonisher's ignorance. Fox knew the Bible almost by heart and used it continually as did nearly all of the early Friends. John Woolman, whose ministry in so many ways affected the middle period of the American Quaker 18th Century, was a hard reader all of his days and the library that he left at his death shows the breadth of his mind and interest. The grasp of poetry and literature that men like John Wilhelm Rowntree and Rufus Jones possessed, far from weakening, seems to have strengthened what they had to give when it was put at the disposal of a deeper guiding. God takes what we have whether it is five loaves or seven or seventy and increases it for the feeding of the hungry. But learning is no substitute for the authentic tendering that takes place in the heart of a gathered meeting.

One of the greatest Christians I ever knew was Henry T. Hodgkin, an English Friend, a medical doctor, a Christian scholar, and the first Director of Pendle Hill. He read widely and deeply and each morning of his adult life he spent an hour in religious concern—a third given to religious reading, a third to the exercise of prayer, and a third to writing in a journal or day-book. He did not simply record the simple events that happened the previous day but rather used the book to write his mind out on things that had come up in his prayer or reading or situations in which he was involved. His strength in the ministry and as a counselor of human beings may have had little to do with this particular pattern of preparation and others may have very different ways of keeping close to the root, but I have never been able to shake off the conviction that Henry Hodgkin lived as a man who was prepared in private for life in public and that there was a connection between the two that was worth pondering.

The psychology that marked the Quietist period in 18th century American Quakerism, which saw the ideal Quaker minister as a hollow tube or an open trumpet for the Lord to blow through, is one that we have laid aside. Four centuries before this, Jan Ruysbroeck, the Flemish mystic, put the matter ever so close to the way we should regard it today when he said, "The love of Jesus is both avid and generous. All that he was and all that he had, he gave; and all that we are and all that we have, he takes." It is precisely so in the vocal ministry in an unprogrammed meeting. But it can be added, that whatever gifts or sufferings or prayer-life or training or insights or learning this master takes, he mercifully transforms them and draws them into his service in another state than he found them.

My own experience is that the gathered meeting provides a nurturing ground for effective ministry. It is such a precious instrument that I have often suggested to ministers in other denominations that if they could get their communities to gather for half an hour before the service and persuade these groups to hold their minister in the atomic-pile of this kind of corporate gathered silence in which whatever message they had brought might be remade and requickened for the group's use, it might revolutionize their whole service of worship. I also would join with those who would encourage Quaker pastors to lengthen materially the scant five minutes they often give for free "communion" when, in the silence, any in the meeting may pray or minister. This lengthened season of gathering might tender the meeting, and open it for the Guide to work in their own subsequent message or perhaps in some word that might be freely spoken from the body of the meeting.

I have said nothing here about the use of vocal prayer in the meeting. Coming early in the meeting or at its close or in some critical point in the exercise, it can enfold the meeting and do much to open it to the Guide. There are too few today who feel the courage to make use of it and it is certainly better to have none than to have it as a mere formality. It may reappear one of these days for our strengthening.

We have received from our Quaker heritage this free ministry that emerges from our corporate waiting on God in what it is not sacrilegious to call a kind of "laboratory of the Holy Spirit." I hope that we may be true to it and may fulfill the conditions of its creative continuance. For it is a gift that far from being outdated is psychologically and spiritually well in advance of its time. If we are true to it, it will bless our lives; it will help to make our own community more truly redemptive; and it is something that we may be able to offer to the ecumenical Christian treasury that may in the future be seen as a gift whose usefulness is beyond measure.